PRINCEWILL LAGANG

Direct from Dell: The Entrepreneurial Journey of Michael Dell

Contents

1

Introduction - Dell: The Entrepreneurial Odyssey

In the ever-evolving landscape of technology and entrepreneurship, the story of Dell Inc. unfolds as an odyssey guided by the visionary spirit of its founder, Michael Dell. This fictional narrative draws inspiration from the real-life journey of one of the tech industry's pioneers, weaving a tale that navigates through the pivotal chapters of innovation, resilience, and a commitment to positive global impact.

In the opening chapters, we venture into the formative moments of Michael Dell's entrepreneurial journey, where the seed of a revolutionary idea takes root in a university dorm room. The narrative explores the genesis of the direct-to-consumer model and the early challenges faced by the ambitious entrepreneur.

As the story progresses, we delve into the dot-com boom, witnessing Dell's ascent as a key player in the tech industry. The narrative unfolds stories of adaptation and strategic innovation, marking the company's response to the dynamic forces shaping the business landscape.

The journey then takes us into the era of mobile technology, cloud computing, and the challenges posed by the dot-com bubble burst. We witness Dell's resilience in reinventing itself, navigating through uncharted waters to emerge stronger and more adaptable.

Chapters dedicated to cybersecurity, sustainability, and global expansion highlight Dell's commitment to ethical business practices and a responsible approach to technology. The narrative envisions Dell not only as a tech giant but as a global emissary, actively contributing to positive change on a worldwide scale.

The odyssey continues into the digital transformation era, exploring Dell's role in shaping the next frontier of technology. The narrative anticipates the company's embrace of emerging technologies, its commitment to sustainability, and its pivotal role in fostering a global tech ecosystem.

As the chapters unfold, readers are invited to reflect on the broader implications of Dell's journey — a journey that transcends individual chapters, leaving an indelible mark on the past, present, and future of technology and entrepreneurship.

Join us on this imaginative venture into the world of Dell, where innovation knows no bounds, and the entrepreneurial spirit propels the narrative beyond the limits of the known into the uncharted territories of tomorrow.

2

A Dorm Room Revelation

Michael Dell's journey began in the unlikeliest of places—a cramped, cluttered dorm room at the University of Texas. It was a room that smelled of ambition, a room where the seeds of entrepreneurship were about to be sown.

Setting the Scene

The year was 1983. The campus hummed with the energy of academia, but for Michael, textbooks and lectures weren't enough. His mind buzzed with the idea of something greater—something that would change the way people interacted with technology.

The Spark of Innovation

Late one night, amidst the dim glow of his computer screen, Michael had a revelation. The clunky, expensive computers of the time could be streamlined and made more accessible. Why wait for innovation when he could bring it directly to the people?

The Birth of an Idea

Armed with determination and a relentless work ethic, Michael began sketching out his vision. The dorm room, once a haven for late-night study sessions, transformed into a makeshift workshop. Circuit boards and cables sprawled across the desk, a visual representation of the chaos that precedes creation.

Late-Night Epiphanies

The campus might have been asleep, but Michael's mind was wide awake. Late into the night, he mapped out his entrepreneurial journey. What began as a vague concept started taking shape—a company that cut through the layers of traditional distribution, selling computers directly to consumers.

The Dorm Room Pitch

The next challenge was convincing others that his idea wasn't just a dream but a revolutionary concept. Friends and classmates gathered in that cramped room, listening intently as Michael passionately articulated his vision. It was more than a product; it was a philosophy—a direct connection between the innovator and the user.

A Leap of Faith

As the first chapter of Michael's journey unfolded, a decision loomed—stay within the safe confines of academia or take a leap into the unpredictable world of business. The dorm room, once a sanctuary of academia, became the birthplace of a daring venture.

The journey was set in motion. Direct from Dell, an entrepreneurial odyssey was about to begin—one that would reshape the tech industry and inspire future generations of innovators.

3

From Garage to Gateway

As Michael Dell embarked on his entrepreneurial journey, the road ahead was uncertain, and challenges loomed like shadows in the night. Chapter 2 dives into the nascent stages of Dell's evolution, where a garage in Austin, Texas, became the crucible for innovation and resilience.

The Garage Workshop

With the first glimmers of success, Michael moved operations from his dorm room to a small garage. It wasn't much, but it was the birthplace of the company. The air was filled with the scent of ambition as a handful of dedicated individuals transformed the modest space into a workshop, assembling computers by hand.

Assembling the Team

Recognizing that he couldn't go it alone, Michael began assembling a team of like-minded individuals who shared his vision. The garage buzzed with the collaborative spirit of passionate innovators, each contributing a unique skill to the growing venture.

Challenges and Triumphs

The early days were far from smooth. Financial constraints, technical glitches, and the skepticism of traditional business models created hurdles. Yet, within these challenges lay the seeds of triumph. Each setback became a stepping stone, pushing the team to refine their approach and build a resilient foundation.

The Direct Model Unveiled

Chapter 2 reveals the unveiling of Dell's revolutionary "direct model." No intermediaries, no middlemen—just a direct line from production to consumer. It was a radical departure from industry norms, challenging the status quo and setting the stage for a paradigm shift in the way technology was bought and sold.

Scaling Heights

Word of the direct model spread, attracting attention beyond the confines of the garage. Small-scale success stories transformed into a burgeoning business. Michael Dell's entrepreneurial spirit and commitment to quality propelled the company forward, scaling heights that seemed unimaginable in those early days.

Lessons Learned

Amidst the victories and defeats, lessons were learned. Chapter 2 reflects on the wisdom gained from navigating the unpredictable terrain of entrepreneurship. Michael Dell and his team discovered the value of adaptability, resilience, and a relentless focus on customer satisfaction.

From Garage to Gateway

As the chapter concludes, the garage that once housed a handful of dreamers now stood as a gateway to a new era in technology. The journey was far from over, but the garage had become a symbol—a testament to the power of innovation, collaboration, and the audacity to challenge convention.

The narrative unfolds, tracing the path from humble beginnings to the cusp of industry transformation. In the garage, the seeds of a tech giant had taken root, ready to blossom into a global force.

4

Navigating Turbulence: Dot-Com Boom and Bust

As Dell Inc. gained momentum in the tech landscape, Chapter 3 delves into a period of exhilarating highs and gut-wrenching lows. The dot-com boom presented unprecedented opportunities, but with it came challenges that tested the resilience of Michael Dell's vision.

Riding the Dot-Com Wave

The late 1990s marked the peak of the dot-com boom, and Dell found itself riding the crest of this technological wave. Demand for personal computers soared, and the direct model proved to be a strategic advantage. Dell became synonymous with the democratization of technology, as consumers and businesses alike flocked to its customizable and affordable products.

Expanding Horizons

With success came expansion. Dell broadened its product offerings, venturing into servers, storage, and services. The once-modest garage operation transformed into a global enterprise. Ambition fueled acquisitions, partnerships, and a relentless pursuit of innovation.

Challenges of Growth

However, the rapid expansion brought its own set of challenges. The company faced increased competition, logistical complexities, and the need for a more diverse set of skills. Chapter 3 explores the internal and external pressures that accompanied Dell's ascent, emphasizing the delicate balance between maintaining a nimble entrepreneurial spirit and managing a corporate giant.

The Bursting Bubble

As the dot-com bubble burst at the turn of the millennium, the tech industry faced a harsh reality check. Chapter 3 narrates how Dell navigated the fallout. Stock prices fluctuated, and the company confronted the need for strategic adjustments. The direct model, once a beacon of success, faced scrutiny in a changing economic landscape.

Reinvention and Resilience

In the face of adversity, Michael Dell and his team displayed resilience. The chapter unfolds the story of reinvention—how Dell re-evaluated its strategies, streamlined operations, and adapted to a market in flux. The focus on customer-centric innovation remained unwavering, anchoring the company amidst the storm.

Learning from Setbacks

Chapter 3 concludes with lessons learned from the turbulence of the dot-com era. Setbacks were not seen as failures but as opportunities for growth. The chapter reflects on the importance of agility, strategic foresight, and the ability to weather storms in the ever-evolving landscape of the tech industry.

A New Dawn

As the dust settled, Dell emerged from the dot-com tumult with a renewed sense of purpose. The narrative transitions to a new era—a post-boom landscape where the company's resilience and commitment to its core values would set the stage for the next chapter in Michael Dell's entrepreneurial journey.

The journey continues, with each twist and turn revealing the enduring spirit that propels Dell forward into uncharted territories.

5

Reinventing the Future: Dell's Leap into the Mobile Age

I n the aftermath of the dot-com turbulence, Dell Inc. faced a world reshaped by technological advancements. Chapter 4 explores the company's strategic pivot into the mobile age, a transformative period where handheld devices became the heartbeat of the digital era.

Winds of Change

As the 21st century unfolded, the tech landscape witnessed a seismic shift towards mobility. Chapter 4 opens with the realization that the future lay not just in desktops and servers, but in the palms of people's hands. Michael Dell, always attuned to industry trends, recognized the winds of change and set a course for innovation.

The Mobile Revolution

Dell embraced the challenge of entering the mobile market head-on. The chapter chronicles the company's foray into smartphones and tablets, navigating the complexities of design, manufacturing, and the intricacies of the mobile ecosystem. The vision was not just to follow trends but to shape them.

Striking the Right Balance

Balancing the legacy of a direct model with the demands of a rapidly evolving market posed a formidable challenge. Chapter 4 explores how Dell sought equilibrium—maintaining its commitment to customization and direct customer engagement while adapting to the fast-paced, dynamic nature of the mobile industry.

Collaborations and Controversies

Partnerships and collaborations became instrumental in Dell's mobile strategy. The chapter unfolds stories of alliances with software giants, as well as the controversies and setbacks that accompanied these ventures. Through collaborations and conflicts, Dell continued to navigate the uncharted waters of mobility.

Lessons in Innovation

The mobile age demanded a fresh perspective on innovation. Chapter 4 showcases how Dell fostered a culture of continuous experimentation, learning from both successes and failures. The company's ability to pivot swiftly, embracing emerging technologies and user trends, became a hallmark of its resilience.

The Human Touch in a Digital World

Amidst the whirlwind of technological advancements, Chapter 4 highlights how Michael Dell remained committed to putting the human touch back into technology. Customer experience and satisfaction were paramount, aligning with the company's ethos from its early days.

Looking Beyond Tomorrow

As Chapter 4 concludes, Dell stands at the intersection of tradition and transformation. The leap into the mobile age not only reshaped the company but also underscored its ability to reinvent, adapt, and stay ahead of the curve. The stage is set for a future where Dell's entrepreneurial journey continues, fueled by a commitment to innovation and a steadfast focus on the evolving needs of its customers.

6

The Resurgence: Dell's Evolution in the Cloud Era

As the technological landscape continued to evolve, Chapter 5 delves into Dell's resurgence in the era of cloud computing. This chapter unfolds a narrative of adaptation, strategic alliances, and the repositioning of Dell as a key player in the dynamic world of cloud technology.

Cloud Computing: A Paradigm Shift

At the dawn of the cloud era, Michael Dell foresaw a fundamental shift in how businesses and individuals would approach computing. Chapter 5 opens with the recognition that the cloud wasn't just a buzzword but a transformative force reshaping the very foundations of IT infrastructure.

Embracing the Cloud

Dell embarked on a strategic journey to embrace cloud computing. The chapter explores how the company pivoted its product and service offerings to align with the demands of a cloud-centric world. From hardware solutions to integrated cloud services, Dell's evolution mirrored the industry's shift towards virtualization and flexibility.

Strategic Acquisitions and Innovations

The narrative unfolds with tales of strategic acquisitions and innovations. Dell's commitment to staying at the forefront of technology is exemplified through stories of acquiring cloud-based startups, developing cutting-edge solutions, and forging partnerships that position the company as a leader in the cloud computing landscape.

The Hybrid Cloud Vision

Chapter 5 highlights the formulation of Dell's hybrid cloud vision—a delicate balance between on-premises infrastructure and cloud-based solutions. The company recognized that the future lay in providing customers with the flexibility to navigate seamlessly between traditional data centers and the vast possibilities of the cloud.

Challenges and Triumphs

The transition to the cloud was not without its challenges. Chapter 5 unfolds the obstacles faced by Dell, from technological complexities to the competitive nature of the cloud market. However, each challenge became an opportunity for innovation, reinforcing Dell's ability to adapt and thrive in the face of adversity.

Customer-Centric Cloud Solutions

Amidst the technological intricacies, the chapter emphasizes Dell's unwavering commitment to delivering customer-centric solutions. From small businesses to multinational corporations, Dell positioned itself as a trusted partner, providing tailored cloud solutions that met the diverse needs of its global clientele.

Future Horizons

As Chapter 5 concludes, Dell stands as a reinvigorated force in the ever-evolving landscape of technology. The cloud era has not only rejuvenated the company but also positioned it as a key influencer in shaping the future of computing. The entrepreneurial journey of Michael Dell and Dell Inc. continues, with the cloud serving as a stepping stone toward new horizons and untapped potentials.

7

Navigating the Digital Frontier: Dell's Role in Cybersecurity

In the midst of a rapidly digitizing world, Chapter 6 unfolds the saga of Dell's entrance into the realm of cybersecurity. As the digital frontier expanded, Michael Dell recognized the critical need to safeguard data and infrastructure, leading the company into uncharted territories fraught with challenges and opportunities.

The Digital Revolution Unleashed

As society became more interconnected, the digital landscape transformed into a playground for innovation and, inevitably, a battleground for cybersecurity threats. Chapter 6 opens with the realization that safeguarding information and networks had become paramount in the age of data.

A Strategic Pivot

Dell's foray into cybersecurity was not just a response to emerging threats but a strategic pivot towards offering comprehensive solutions. The chapter explores how the company evolved its product and service portfolio to encompass cybersecurity, recognizing that protecting data was integral to its mission of empowering individuals and organizations.

Building Fortresses: Dell's Security Solutions

From firewalls to advanced threat detection systems, Chapter 6 delves into the development of Dell's security solutions. The company positioned itself as a guardian of digital fortresses, offering not only hardware but also cutting-edge software designed to thwart cyber threats at every level.

The Human Element of Cybersecurity

Amidst the technological intricacies, Dell embraced the human element of cybersecurity. The narrative highlights the company's commitment to educating users, promoting cybersecurity awareness, and empowering organizations to build a robust human firewall against evolving threats.

Partnerships and Collaborations

Recognizing the complexity of the cybersecurity landscape, Chapter 6 unveils stories of strategic partnerships and collaborations. Dell joined forces with industry leaders, cybersecurity experts, and government agencies to create a united front against cyber threats, fostering a collaborative ecosystem focused on collective defense.

Ethical Dilemmas and Privacy Concerns

The chapter doesn't shy away from exploring the ethical dilemmas and privacy concerns associated with cybersecurity. Dell faced scrutiny and challenges in navigating the fine line between protecting user data and respecting individual privacy rights, sparking debates that resonated far beyond the confines of the tech industry.

Securing the Future

As Chapter 6 draws to a close, Dell stands as a vanguard in the digital security landscape. The company's journey into cybersecurity not only reflects its commitment to innovation but also its responsibility as a global tech leader. The entrepreneurial spirit that guided Michael Dell through previous chapters continues to drive Dell Inc. forward, securing not just data but also the trust of millions in the ever-evolving digital frontier.

8

Dell's Sustainable Odyssey: Navigating the Green Tech Seas

As the world grappled with the consequences of climate change, Chapter 7 unveils Dell's commitment to sustainability and its journey toward becoming a leader in green technology. Michael Dell's vision extended beyond innovation and profit, embracing the responsibility to create a tech ecosystem that balanced progress with environmental stewardship.

The Call of Sustainability

Amidst growing environmental concerns, the chapter begins with Michael Dell's recognition of the need for a sustainable approach to technology. The narrative explores the moment when the call for environmental responsibility became a driving force, steering Dell toward a new mission: to create technology that not only advances humanity but also preserves the planet.

Reducing the Carbon Footprint

Dell's commitment to sustainability takes center stage as the company explores ways to reduce its carbon footprint. Chapter 7 delves into the development of eco-friendly manufacturing processes, energy-efficient products, and a comprehensive strategy to minimize the environmental impact of its operations.

Circular Economy: Closing the Loop

A key theme of the chapter is Dell's embrace of the circular economy—a model that aims to minimize waste by recycling and reusing materials. From product design to end-of-life disposal, Dell's journey unfolds as the company strives to create a closed-loop system, minimizing its contribution to electronic waste.

Renewable Energy Initiatives

Chapter 7 chronicles Dell's initiatives to harness the power of renewable energy. From solar farms to innovative energy-efficient data centers, the company explores ways to transition to a more sustainable energy model. The narrative emphasizes Dell's commitment to not only neutralize its environmental impact but also contribute positively to the global energy landscape.

The Challenges of Green Innovation

The chapter doesn't shy away from the challenges of green innovation. Dell faces technological, economic, and logistical hurdles on the path to sustainability. The narrative unfolds stories of setbacks and triumphs as Dell strives to balance the demands of a rapidly evolving tech industry with the imperative to protect the planet.

Beyond Profit: The Social Impact

As sustainability becomes a core value, Chapter 7 explores Dell's endeavors to make a positive social impact. The company invests in community initiatives, education programs, and partnerships that extend the benefits of technology to underserved populations, creating a holistic approach that transcends traditional profit-driven models.

A Legacy of Responsibility

As Chapter 7 concludes, Dell's sustainability journey stands as a testament to its commitment to responsible business practices. Michael Dell's vision of a green tech future has not only transformed the company but has also set a standard for the industry. The chapter closes with the understanding that Dell's odyssey in sustainability is an ongoing venture, an integral part of the larger narrative of responsible entrepreneurship and a commitment to leaving a positive impact on the world.

9

Dell 4.0 - The Digital Transformation Symphony

In Chapter 8, the narrative unfolds as Dell embraces the era of digital transformation, navigating a landscape where technology is not just a tool but a catalyst for fundamental change. Michael Dell's vision extends beyond hardware and sustainability, propelling Dell Inc. into a new frontier where data, artificial intelligence, and connectivity redefine the very essence of innovation.

The Digital Imperative

As the 21st century unfolds, the chapter begins with the realization that digital transformation is not a choice but a necessity. Dell acknowledges that the future is data-driven, and the ability to harness the power of information will be the key to success in a rapidly evolving digital ecosystem.

Building Intelligent Systems

Chapter 8 explores Dell's role in building intelligent systems that go beyond traditional computing. The narrative unfolds with stories of AI integration, machine learning applications, and the development of solutions that empower businesses to not only process vast amounts of data but derive meaningful insights that drive innovation.

Edge Computing and Connectivity

A central theme of the chapter is the rise of edge computing and the importance of seamless connectivity. Dell's journey includes the exploration of technologies that push computing capabilities closer to the source of data, enhancing efficiency, reducing latency, and laying the groundwork for a more connected and responsive world.

The Cybersecurity Continuum

In the era of digital transformation, cybersecurity takes center stage once again. Chapter 8 delves into how Dell adapts its security strategies to combat sophisticated cyber threats in a hyper-connected world. The narrative reflects the continuous evolution of security measures to safeguard not only data but also the intricate web of interconnected devices.

Empowering the Remote Workforce

The chapter unfolds against the backdrop of a shifting work paradigm. Dell embraces the challenges and opportunities presented by the rise of remote work, developing solutions that empower a distributed workforce while addressing the security and connectivity concerns inherent in this new professional landscape.

Customer-Centric Design in the Digital Age

Chapter 8 emphasizes the continued importance of customer-centric design. Dell not only adapts its products and services to the digital age but also focuses on user experience, ensuring that technological advancements translate into practical solutions that meet the evolving needs and expectations of its diverse clientele.

From Digitization to Transformation

As Chapter 8 concludes, Dell stands at the forefront of the digital transformation wave. The narrative reflects not just a digitization of processes but a fundamental transformation—a shift in mindset, culture, and approach that propels Dell Inc. into a new era of technological leadership.

The journey continues, as Michael Dell and Dell Inc. navigate the ever-accelerating pace of digital innovation, contributing to a future where technology is not just a tool but a force for positive change in the world.

10

Dell Beyond Boundaries - A Global Tech Emissary

As Dell Inc. continues its journey into the future, Chapter 9 unfolds a narrative of global expansion, cultural integration, and the company's role as a tech emissary on the world stage. Michael Dell's vision extends beyond borders, embracing the challenges and opportunities presented by a interconnected and diverse global landscape.

Bridging Continents: Dell's Global Expansion

The chapter opens with the story of Dell's expansion beyond its American roots. Dell becomes a global player, establishing a presence on multiple continents. The narrative explores the challenges of cultural diversity, international market dynamics, and the strategic decisions that position Dell as a truly global tech enterprise.

Tech for Good: Dell's Global Impact

Beyond profit margins, Chapter 9 delves into Dell's commitment to social responsibility on a global scale. The company initiates programs and partnerships that leverage technology to address pressing global issues, from education and healthcare to environmental sustainability. The narrative reflects on Dell's role as a force for positive change in diverse communities around the world.

Cultural Integration and Diversity

Navigating the global landscape requires an understanding and appreciation of diverse cultures. Chapter 9 explores how Dell fosters a culture of inclusion, diversity, and collaboration. The narrative reflects on the importance of a global workforce that brings together perspectives from different backgrounds, enriching the company's innovation and problem-solving capabilities.

Adapting to Regulatory Landscapes

As Dell expands globally, the chapter delves into the complexities of navigating diverse regulatory environments. From compliance challenges to ethical considerations, Dell's journey reflects the company's commitment to conducting business with integrity and respect for local laws and customs.

Global Partnerships and Collaborations

The narrative unfolds with stories of strategic partnerships and collaborations that transcend borders. Dell engages with governments, businesses, and organizations worldwide to drive technological advancements that have a positive impact on a global scale. The chapter emphasizes Dell's role as a collaborative force in shaping the international tech landscape.

Resilience in a Global Context

Chapter 9 reflects on the resilience required to thrive in a global context.

Economic shifts, geopolitical challenges, and unforeseen global events test Dell's adaptability and strategic foresight. The narrative unfolds stories of triumphs over adversity and lessons learned in the pursuit of sustainable global growth.

A Global Vision for Tomorrow

As Chapter 9 concludes, Dell stands as a global tech emissary with a vision that extends beyond individual nations. The narrative looks toward the future, where Dell Inc. continues to evolve as a company that not only adapts to the intricacies of a connected world but also actively contributes to shaping a positive and inclusive global technological future.

11

Dell's Odyssey Continues - The Next Frontier

I n the final chapter of this entrepreneurial odyssey, the narrative unfolds as Dell Inc. faces the challenges and embraces the opportunities of the next frontier. Michael Dell's journey, marked by innovation, resilience, and a commitment to customer-centric values, extends into a future where the only constant is change.

The Tech Horizon Unveiled

Chapter 10 opens with a glimpse into the horizon of emerging technologies. Dell Inc. positions itself at the forefront of innovations such as quantum computing, augmented reality, and the Internet of Things. The narrative explores how the company adapts its strategies to harness the potential of these transformative technologies.

A Vision for a Sustainable Tomorrow

Building upon the sustainability initiatives of previous chapters, the narrative unfolds Dell's vision for a future where technology not only advances but also sustains the planet. The company continues to pioneer eco-friendly practices, circular economy models, and initiatives that contribute to a greener and more sustainable world.

The Human Element in Technology

In the midst of technological advancements, the chapter emphasizes the enduring importance of the human element. Dell continues to champion user-centric design, ethical considerations in artificial intelligence, and a commitment to ensuring that technology serves humanity rather than the other way around.

Entrepreneurship and Innovation: A Continuum

Chapter 10 reflects on Dell's ongoing commitment to fostering entrepreneurship and innovation. The company invests in start-ups, incubators, and educational initiatives that nurture the next generation of visionaries. The narrative unfolds stories of collaboration and mentorship, underscoring Dell's role as a guiding force in the ever-evolving tech landscape.

Legacy and Future Horizons

As Michael Dell's entrepreneurial journey approaches a new phase, the chapter reflects on the legacy of Dell Inc. The narrative explores how the values ingrained in the company's DNA—innovation, customer focus, sustainability, and global responsibility—continue to guide its trajectory into the future.

Adapting to Unknowns

The final chapter acknowledges that the future is rife with unknowns. Technological, economic, and social landscapes will undoubtedly shift.

Chapter 10 explores how Dell Inc. prepares for uncertainties, leveraging the lessons of the past to navigate uncharted territories with agility and foresight.

The Entrepreneurial Spirit Lives On

As Chapter 10 draws to a close, the narrative leaves the door ajar for the next chapters in Dell's story. The entrepreneurial spirit that fueled Michael Dell's journey remains a driving force, propelling Dell Inc. into a future where innovation, responsibility, and a commitment to positive global impact continue to shape the company's destiny.

The odyssey continues, and the story of Dell Inc. stands as a testament to the enduring power of entrepreneurial vision in the ever-evolving landscape of technology.

12

Dell's Ever-Evolving Legacy - The Ripple Effect

In this epilogue chapter, we reflect on the enduring legacy of Dell Inc. as it continues to shape the world of technology and business. The narrative weaves through the impact of Michael Dell's journey, exploring how the company's innovations, values, and commitment to positive change have created a ripple effect across industries and societies.

The Transformative Ripple

Chapter 11 begins by tracing the transformative ripple that emanates from Dell's journey. The chapter explores how the company's revolutionary ideas, from the direct model to sustainability practices, have influenced not only its competitors but the broader tech industry. Dell's journey becomes a case study in the power of entrepreneurship to drive systemic change.

From Start-Up to Standard-Bearer

Reflecting on the path from a dorm room operation to a global tech standard-bearer, the narrative unfolds stories of perseverance, adaptability, and the ability to stay true to core values. Dell's evolution becomes a testament to the enduring impact of a visionary leader and a dedicated team.

A Beacon of Responsibility

Chapter 11 delves into Dell's role as a beacon of responsibility in the corporate world. The company's commitment to sustainability, diversity, and ethical business practices sets a standard for responsible entrepreneurship. The narrative reflects on how Dell's journey inspires other businesses to integrate social and environmental responsibility into their core strategies.

Nurturing Future Visionaries

As Dell Inc. continues to thrive, the narrative explores the company's efforts to nurture and support the next generation of visionaries. Dell becomes not just a company but a mentor, investing in educational programs, incubators, and initiatives that empower future leaders to shape the technological landscape with responsibility and innovation.

The Human Impact

Beyond the boardroom and balance sheets, Chapter 11 explores the human impact of Dell's journey. The company's products and services have touched the lives of millions, transforming the way people work, connect, and live. The narrative unfolds stories of individuals and communities positively impacted by Dell's technologies.

A Living Legacy

The chapter reflects on how Michael Dell's entrepreneurial journey and the legacy of Dell Inc. are living entities, continually evolving and responding to the dynamic nature of technology and society. The narrative suggests that the company's legacy is not a static endpoint but an ongoing narrative, with each chapter influencing the next.

The Unwritten Future

As Chapter 11 concludes, the narrative looks toward the unwritten future. Dell's journey becomes a part of the broader narrative of technological advancement, responsible business practices, and the ever-expanding possibilities of the digital age. The entrepreneurial spirit that initiated this odyssey remains an eternal flame, lighting the way for the next chapters yet to be written.

The legacy endures, and the ripple effect of Dell's journey continues to shape the world, leaving an indelible mark on the past, present, and future of technology and entrepreneurship.

13

Dell Beyond Tomorrow - Embracing the Uncharted

In this final chapter, we embark on a contemplative journey that looks beyond the immediate horizon, exploring the unwritten chapters of Dell's story. Chapter 12 envisions a future where Dell Inc. continues to be a trailblazer, embracing the uncharted territories of technology, business, and global impact.

The Visionary Compass

As we step into the future, the narrative explores how Michael Dell's visionary compass remains at the heart of Dell Inc. The chapter reflects on the enduring principles that have guided the company through decades of innovation and adaptation, providing a foundation for the journeys yet to unfold.

A Symphony of Technologies

Chapter 12 envisions a technological symphony where Dell continues to play a leading role. From quantum computing to advancements in artificial intelligence, the narrative unfolds stories of Dell's contributions to the ever-evolving technological landscape. The company becomes a symphony conductor, orchestrating innovations that resonate globally.

Tech with Purpose

The narrative delves into the concept of "tech with purpose." Dell Inc. becomes a driving force behind technology that not only transforms industries but also addresses pressing global challenges. The company's initiatives extend beyond profit, contributing to a future where technology becomes a catalyst for positive change.

Shaping the Future Workforce

Chapter 12 reflects on Dell's role in shaping the future workforce. The company becomes a protagonist in the narrative of education and skill development, empowering individuals to thrive in the digital age. Dell's initiatives aim to bridge the digital divide, ensuring that the benefits of technology are accessible to all.

Redefining Connectivity

The narrative envisions a world where connectivity is not just about devices but about fostering meaningful connections. Dell becomes a facilitator of global connectivity, enabling collaboration and communication across borders. The chapter explores how Dell's technologies contribute to a more interconnected and empathetic world.

Ethical Tech Leadership

As the tech landscape evolves, Chapter 12 emphasizes Dell's commitment to ethical tech leadership. The narrative reflects on the company's role in guiding industry practices, advocating for responsible AI, data privacy, and ethical business conduct. Dell becomes a beacon for others, setting standards that prioritize humanity over profit.

The Uncharted Territories

The chapter concludes by embracing the uncertainty of the uncharted territories. Dell's journey becomes a dynamic narrative, open to the unpredictable twists and turns of the evolving world. The company stands ready to navigate the unknown, armed with the entrepreneurial spirit that has been the hallmark of its story.

A Never-Ending Odyssey

As we close the final chapter, the narrative leaves the door open for the never-ending odyssey of Dell Inc. The company's story continues, shaped by the hands of visionaries, innovators, and a global community that looks to the future with anticipation. Dell's odyssey is not just a story; it's an invitation to imagine, innovate, and embrace the infinite possibilities of the uncharted.

14

Summary

"Dell: The Entrepreneurial Odyssey" is a multi-chapter fictional narrative tracing the evolution of Dell Inc. inspired by Michael Dell's entrepreneurial journey. The story begins in a dorm room, where Michael Dell envisions a direct-to-consumer model for computers. It then chronicles the company's growth, challenges, and triumphs through various chapters, touching on the dot-com era, mobile technology, cloud computing, cybersecurity, sustainability, global expansion, and the digital transformation.

Each chapter explores pivotal moments, lessons learned, and the company's response to industry shifts. The narrative emphasizes Dell's commitment to innovation, customer-centricity, sustainability, and social responsibility. It envisions Dell as a global tech emissary, navigating the challenges of each era while leaving a positive impact on the world.

The story concludes with chapters envisioning Dell's role in emerging technologies, its commitment to ethical leadership, and the uncharted territories of the future. The legacy of Dell Inc. is portrayed as an ongoing narrative, shaped by visionary leadership and the ever-evolving landscape of technology. The narrative invites readers to reflect on the broader implications of Dell's journey and anticipate the company's future contributions to the dynamic world of entrepreneurship and technology.

39

www.ingramcontent.com/pod-product-compliance
Lightning Source LLC
LaVergne TN
LVHW051242200726
843510LV00011B/1653